A Little Catholic's First
ROSARY BOOK

The Sorrowful Mysteries

A Bead-by-Bead Picture Prayer Book

By Sandra Rosetter
Illustrations by Stacey LeNeave

www.HolyHeroes.com

The Sorrowful Mysteries

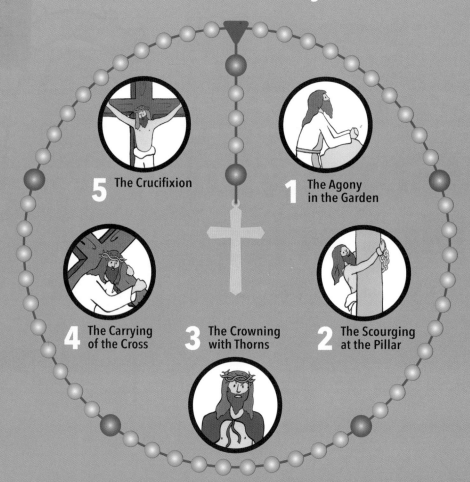

5 The Crucifixion

1 The Agony in the Garden

4 The Carrying of the Cross

3 The Crowning with Thorns

2 The Scourging at the Pillar

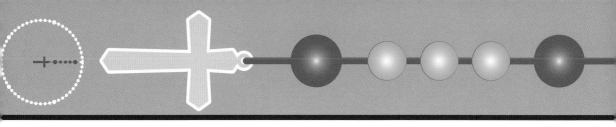

In the name of the Father ...

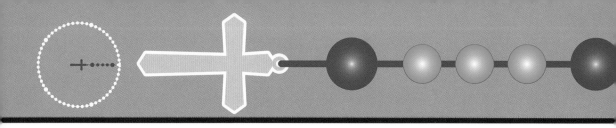

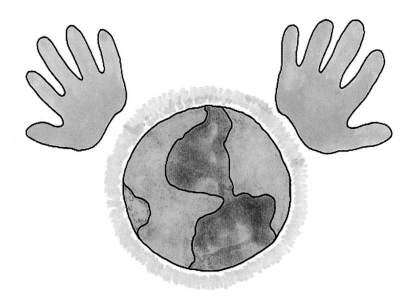

Apostles' Creed

Our Father ...

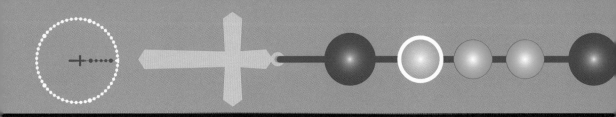

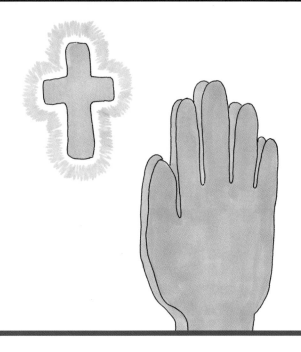

For an increase in
the virtue of Faith

Hail, Mary ...

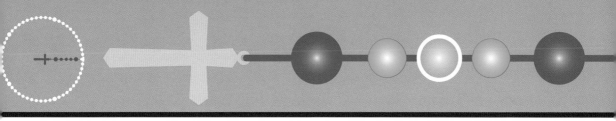

For an increase in
the virtue of Hope

Hail, Mary ...

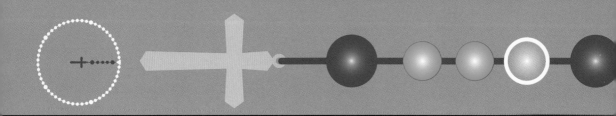

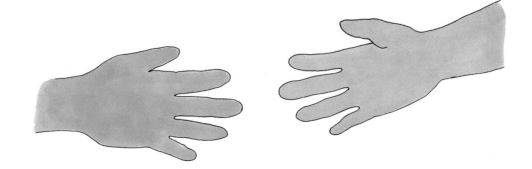

For an increase in
the virtue of Charity

Hail, Mary ...

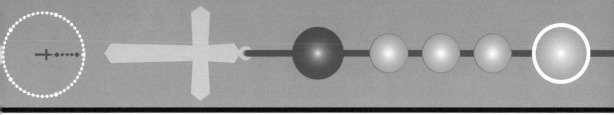

Glory Be ...

The First Sorrowful Mystery is
The Agony in the Garden

Jesus suffers fear and sorrow

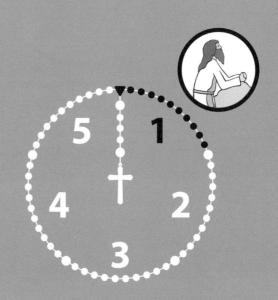

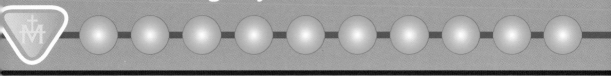

Our Father ...

The Agony in the Garden

Jesus takes Peter, James and John
to the Garden of Gethsemane

Hail, Mary ...

The Agony in the Garden

Jesus is troubled, so He asks them to stay awake with Him

Hail, Mary ...

Jesus walks farther
into the garden to pray

Hail, Mary ...

Jesus asks that He not need to suffer, but He will do whatever God requires

Hail, Mary ...

Jesus finds His Apostles sleeping and asks them to wake up and pray

Hail, Mary ...

Jesus returns again to pray

Hail, Mary ...

God the Father sends an angel
to comfort Jesus

Hail, Mary ...

Jesus returns to find His Apostles
asleep again and awakens them

Hail, Mary ...

Judas and the soldiers arrive

Hail, Mary ...

Judas greets Jesus with a kiss

Hail, Mary ...

Glory Be ...

Oh My Jesus ...

The Second Sorrowful Mystery is

The Scourging at the Pillar

The soldiers whip Jesus

Our Father ...

Instead of Jesus, the crowd chooses Barabbas to be set free

Hail, Mary ...

Pilate says Jesus is not guilty,
but has Him whipped anyway

Hail, Mary ...

The soldiers lead Jesus
to the pillar

Hail, Mary ...

They strip Him of His garments

Hail, Mary ...

The soldiers tie Jesus
to the pillar

Hail, Mary ...

They take turns whipping Him

Hail, Mary ...

Jesus feels the pain,
but does not cry out

Hail, Mary ...

The soldiers continue whipping Him

Hail, Mary ...

Finally, it is over,
and they untie Him

Hail, Mary ...

Jesus is released
and falls to the ground

Hail, Mary ...

Glory Be ...

Oh My Jesus ...

The Third Sorrowful Mystery is
The Crowning with Thorns

Jesus is mocked by the soldiers

Our Father ...

The soldiers lead Jesus away

Hail, Mary ...

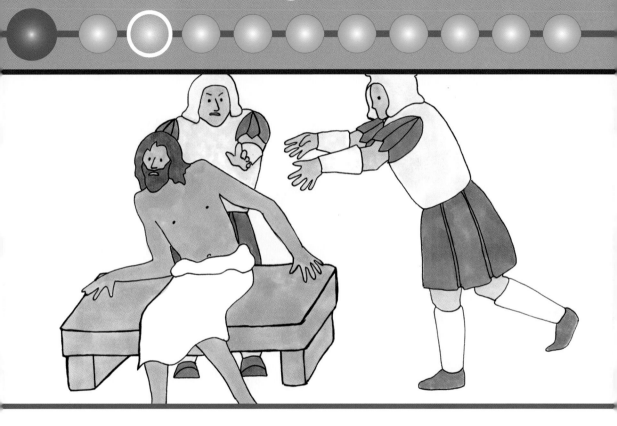

They push Him onto the bench | Hail, Mary ...

They place a purple cloak on Him

Hail, Mary ...

The soldiers mock Jesus
as a "King"

Hail, Mary ...

They hand Him a stick
to be a scepter

Hail, Mary ...

The soldiers decide
Jesus needs a "crown"

Hail, Mary ...

45

They find branches with thorns
to make a crown

Hail, Mary ...

They force it on His head

Hail, Mary ...

The soldiers pretend
to honor Him as a king

Hail, Mary ...

They continue making fun of Him and spit on Him

Hail, Mary ...

Glory Be ...

Oh My Jesus ...

The Fourth Sorrowful Mystery is
The Carrying of the Cross

Jesus carries His Cross to Calvary

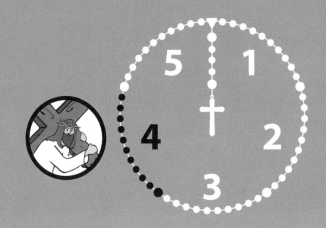

Our Father ...

The heavy Cross
is laid on Jesus' shoulders

Hail, Mary ...

A large crowd follows Jesus

Hail, Mary ...

Jesus falls for the first time

Hail, Mary ...

Jesus is met by Mary, His mother | Hail, Mary ...

Simon of Cyrene is made
to help Jesus carry His Cross

Hail, Mary ...

Veronica wipes the face of Jesus

Hail, Mary ...

Jesus falls the second time

Hail, Mary ...

Jesus speaks to the
women of Jerusalem

Hail, Mary ...

The Carrying of the Cross

Jesus falls for the third time | Hail, Mary ...

Jesus makes His way
up Mount Calvary

Hail, Mary ...

Glory Be ...

Oh My Jesus ...

The Fifth Sorrowful Mystery is
The Crucifixion

Jesus is nailed to the Cross and dies for our sins

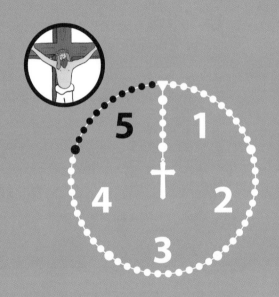

Our Father ...

The soldiers remove
Jesus' garments

Hail, Mary ...

Jesus is thrown down
onto the Cross

Hail, Mary ...

The soldiers nail His hands
and feet to the Cross

Hail, Mary ...

The Cross is lifted up
with Jesus on it

Hail, Mary ...

A sign is placed above His head | Hail, Mary ...

Two criminals are crucified
with Jesus

Hail, Mary ...

Jesus' mother Mary, the Apostle John, and others are at the Cross

Hail, Mary ...

Jesus tells Mary that John will be her son and that she will be his mother

Hail, Mary ...

Jesus gives up His spirit
to God the Father, and dies

Hail, Mary ...

When Jesus dies,
the afternoon sky turns dark

Hail, Mary ...

Glory Be ...

Oh My Jesus ...

Hail, Holy Queen ...

Make the Sign of the Cross

In the name of the Father ...

Prayers of the Rosary

The Sign of the Cross

In the name of the Father, and of the Son, and of the Holy Spirit. Amen.

Our Father (The Lord's Prayer)

Our Father, Who art in Heaven,
hallowed be Thy Name;
Thy Kingdom come,
Thy Will be done on earth as it is in Heaven.
Give us this day our daily bread,
and forgive us our trespasses,
as we forgive those who trespass against us;
And lead us not into temptation,
but deliver us from evil. Amen.

Hail, Mary

Hail, Mary, full of grace,
the Lord is with thee.
Blessed art thou among women,
and blessed is the fruit of thy womb, Jesus.
Holy Mary, Mother of God,
pray for us sinners,
now and at the hour of our death. Amen.

Glory Be

Glory be to the Father,
and to the Son,
and to the Holy Spirit.
As it was in the beginning,
is now, and ever shall be,
world without end. Amen.

Fatima Prayer

Oh my Jesus, forgive us our sins.
Save us from the fires of Hell.
Lead all souls to Heaven, especially those in most need of Thy mercy. Amen.

Apostles' Creed

I believe in God,
the Father almighty,
Creator of Heaven and earth,
and in Jesus Christ, His only Son, our Lord,
who was conceived by the Holy Spirit,
born of the Virgin Mary,
suffered under Pontius Pilate,
was crucified, died and was buried;
He descended into Hell;
on the third day He rose again from the dead;
He ascended into Heaven,
and is seated at the right hand of God
the Father almighty;
from there He will come to judge
the living and the dead.

I believe in the Holy Spirit,
the holy catholic Church,
the communion of saints,
the forgiveness of sins,
the resurrection of the body,
and life everlasting. Amen.

Hail, Holy Queen (Salve Regina)

Hail, Holy Queen,
Mother of Mercy,
our life, our sweetness,
and our hope.
To thee do we cry,
poor banished children of Eve.
To thee do we send up our sighs,
mourning and weeping in this valley of tears.
Turn then, most gracious advocate,
thine eyes of mercy toward us,
and after this, our exile,
show unto us the blessed fruit of thy womb,
Jesus.
O clement, O loving,
O sweet Virgin Mary,
Pray for us, O holy Mother of God,
That we may be made worthy
of the promises of Christ. Amen.

From the Author

These books grew from a desire to help young children remain engaged while praying the Rosary, enabling them to develop a genuine love for this beautiful devotion. To do this, we "tell" the story of each Mystery "Bead by Bead" in ten consecutive pictures: one for each prayer.

The lovely illustrations in these books were created by my talented sister and dear friend, Stacey LeNeave. It is our fond hope that these prayer books help to develop your child's prayer life (and maybe yours, too!).

—Sandy Rosetter

Dedicated, with love, to
Father Brendan Jerry McMullen, OP
(1912–2005)

HOLY HEROES®

Helping You Bring the Joy of the Faith to Your Family

A Little Catholic's Book, published by Holy Heroes, LLC.   **www.HolyHeroes.com**   All rights reserved.   ISBN: 978-1-936330-91-1